ANCIENT CIVILIZATIONS

ANCIENT EGYPT

STEWART ROSS

WORLD ALMANAC® LIBRARY

Please visit our web site at: www.worldalmanaclibrary.com
For a free color catalog describing World Almanac® Library's list of high-quality books and multimedia programs, call 1-800-848-2928 (USA) or 1-800-387-3178 (Canada). World Almanac® Library's fax: (414) 332-3567.

Library of Congress Cataloging-in-Publication Data

Stewart, Ross.
    Ancient Egypt / by Stewart Ross.
      p. cm. — (Ancient civilizations)
    Includes bibliographical references and index.
    ISBN 0-8368-6189-2 (lib. bdg.)
    1. Egypt—Civilization—To 332 B.C.—Juvenile literature. I. Title.
    DT61.R5682   2006
    932—dc22   2005052628

This North American edition first published in 2006 by
World Almanac® Library
A Member of the WRC Media Family of Companies
330 West Olive Street, Suite 100
Milwaukee, WI 53212 USA

This U.S. edition copyright © 2006 by World Almanac® Library. Original edition copyright © 2006 by Hodder Wayland. First published in 2006 by Hodder Wayland, an imprint of Hodder Children's Books, a division of Hodder Headline Limited, 338 Euston Road, London NW1 3BH, U.K.

Project editor: Kirsty Hamilton
Designer: Simon Borrough
Maps: Peter Bull
World Almanac® Library editor: Gini Holland
World Almanac® Library art direction: Tammy West
World Almanac® Library cover design: Dave Kowalski
World Almanac® Library production: Jessica Morris

Picture credits: Gianni Dagli Orti / Corbis, title page, pp. 22 (bottom), 23, 25, 26, 28, 31, 35, 45 (bottom); Francis G. Mayer / Corbis pp. 3, 27, 30; Digital Image © 1996 Corbis / original image courtesy of NASA / Corbis p. 5; Charles & Josette Lenars / Corbis p. 6; Richard T. Nowitz / Corbis p. 7; Paul Almasy / Corbis p. 8; Roger Ressmeyer / Corbis p. 9; Roger Wood / Corbis pp. 11, 43; Carmen Redondo / Corbis p. 12; Dave Bartruff / Corbis p. 13 (top) ; Adam Woolfitt / Corbis p. 13 (bottom); akg images / Andrea Jemolo p. 14; Werner Forman / Corbis p. 15; akg-images / Erich Lessing p. 16; North Carolina Museum of Art / Corbis p. 18; Stapleton Collection / Corbis p. 19; Werner Forman Archive/ E. Strouhal p. 20; Werner Forman Archive / British Museum no.32610 p. 21; Archivo Incongrafico, S.A / Corbis pp. 22 (top), 24, 29, 33, 34, 36, 41; Sandro Vannini / Corbis pp. 32, 37; Bettmann / Corbis pp. 38, 45 (top); akg images / Robert O'Dea p. 39; akg-images / Erich Lessing p. 40; Historical Picture Archive / Corbis p. 44

Printed in China

1 2 3 4 5 6 7 8 9 10 09 08 07 06

CONTENTS

WHO WERE THE ANCIENT EGYPTIANS?

Egypt was home to the longest-lived and perhaps the most startling of all ancient civilizations. Its achievements, especially in art, government, and construction, made Egypt one of the ancient world's most advanced civilizations. Remarkably, though, Egyptian achievements were accomplished in a most unfavorable, hot, and arid environment.

Egypt, still a country today, is a large, mostly barren land in northeast Africa. It is bordered on two sides by seas: the Mediterranean to the north and the Red Sea to the east. To the south is present-day Sudan (ancient Nubia) and, beyond that, the Central African uplands. The western frontier is mostly desert. What binds Egypt together is the mighty Nile River, which flows north downhill for the length of the country before it empties into the Mediterranean Sea.

Stone Age settlers came to the green areas on either bank of this river around 5000 B.C. and set up farming communities. The land was less arid than today, and the communities thrived and expanded into one of the world's great civilizations.

The people of ancient Egypt were not a racially distinct group: The Arabs that make up the bulk of

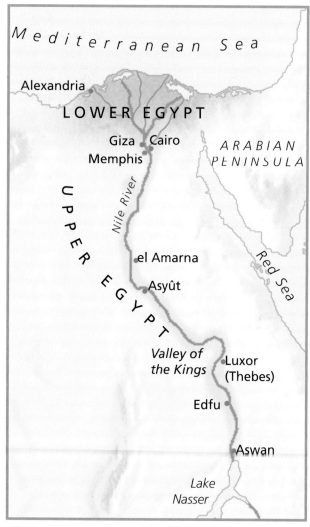

▲ This map shows Ancient Egypt and the Nile River.

Mediterranean Sea
Alexandria
LOWER EGYPT
Giza Cairo
Memphis
ARABIAN PENINSULA
Nile River
UPPER EGYPT
el Amarna
Asyût
Red Sea
Valley of the Kings
Luxor (Thebes)
Edfu
Aswan
Lake Nasser

▲ A view of the delta of the Nile River seen from a satellite in 2003.

modern Egypt were in ancient times mostly confined to the Arabian peninsula. The citizens of ancient Egypt were a mix of African, Mediterranean, and European peoples. They thought of themselves as a distinct civilization because of how they lived, not because of their appearance. In fact, members of several racial groups could be found at all levels of society.

THE NILE

Ancient Egyptian civilization centered around the Nile River. Without the river there would have been no civilization—it was, literally, the Egyptians' river of life.

Before the Aswan Dam was built, late in the twentieth century, rainwater from mountains far to the south poured into the river once a year and caused it to flood along most of its length. This flooding deposited rich silt (soil) along the banks. The flood (or "inundation," around July–September) was one of Egypt's three seasons. The other two were the growing season after the waters had subsided (roughly October–April) and the dry season (May–June).

The inundation was the most important season of the year. By leaving fresh layers of new soil along the Nile's banks, it allowed the Egyptians to grow crops that would not otherwise have survived in the dusty desert. Without the wheat grown along the fertile strip beside the river, settled life for large numbers of people would have been impossible. More than sufficient food was grown, so some was exported. Moreover, the easy farming conditions gave workers spare time in which to work on other projects.

Prayer from *Book of the Dead*

"Hail, Great God! Not once have I blocked up a water channel."

What does it tell us?

The Egyptian *Book of the Dead* was a collection of prayers and utterances intended to help a soul pass to the next world. To gain release, a soul had to show that it had lived a good life and not done wrong. This prayer emphasizes the vital importance of irrigation—bringing water from the river to the fields and holding it there after the inundation. To block a water channel was seen as wicked enough to condemn a soul to eternal misery.

◀ This ancient Egyptian fresco shows a wife sowing seeds while her husband plows the field with oxen.

Ancient water meter

What does it tell us?

Although this looks like a set of steps, it is in fact a Nilometer—a means of measuring the height of the Nile River. The height of the inundation (measured by the height of the water on the central column) was of great importance in ancient Egypt. Some scholars have suggested that taxes (in the form of produce) depended on the height of the water: high flood equals more land irrigated, which means more food grown to bring more taxes.

A great civilization for 3,000 years

What does it tell us?

More than 7,000 years ago, people settled in communities along the fertile banks of the Nile River. About 2,000 years later, these communities were united into the state of Egypt under a single king. For the next 3,000 years, Egypt was one of the richest, most cultured, and best ordered states in the world. Impressive evidence of its past greatness survives in the form of mighty pyramids and temples. Ancient Egyptian power declined in the first millennium B.C. until, in 30 B.C., it was absorbed into the Roman Empire.

The importance of the inundation in ancient Egyptian life was emphasized by the focus on Hapy, the god of the inundation. He was basically a male figure with a potbelly, but he also had large breasts and wore a headdress of plants. These mixed physical attributes made him a fitting symbol of the fertility that is provided by the swelling river.

As well as allowing irrigation for agriculture, the Nile had many other functions. It was almost the only source of drinking water for people and beasts. Numerous fish were caught in it as well. Its reedy banks were home to many birds that Egyptians hunted for food. The reeds themselves were cut, dried, and used for a wide variety of purposes. Finally, the Nile was Egypt's main highway, connecting south to north.

A GREAT CIVILIZATION

Other striking aspects of ancient Egyptian civilization include its duration, the power of its leaders, and its majestic

▲ A sunk relief sculpture of two images of the Nile god Hapy, tying together Upper and Lower Egypt.

monuments. Most impressive of these is the sheer length of time over which it survived, from about 3100 to 30 B.C., or three thousand years. The scale of this survival is clear when compared with the duration of ancient Roman civilization, which was a mere eight hundred years.

Another interesting characteristic of ancient Egypt is the position held by its kings and queens. Rarely have human beings had such power. The king did not just rule the land. He also was feared and even sometimes worshipped as a god. Egyptian royal women had more power and influence than women in other early civilizations.

The parts of ancient Egypt that most people know best are its towering monuments, in particular the Sphinx and Great Pyramid of Giza. These are the most impressive pieces of evidence of the Egyptians' brilliant skills as builders and organizers. The pyramids were royal burial sites in which everything monarchs might need in the afterlife was buried with them. Because they were essentially religious monuments, the pyramids are a vivid reminder of the central part religion played in Egyptians' lives.

The most magnificent evidence of all

What does it tell us?

The Great Pyramid of Giza (*below, right*), one of the wonders of the world, was built some 4,500 years ago. It is a mine of information about ancient Egypt. Precisely constructed from 3.2 million blocks of limestone weighing an average 2.76 tons (2.5 tonnes) each, the Great Pyramid leaves us staggered by the skills and organization of the people who carved out these blocks so accurately, moved them to the building site, and fitted them together so precisely. Its function as a royal burial chamber that points to the sky is strong evidence of the importance and power of the king who ordered it to be built (Khufu, 2589–2566 B.C.) and the primary importance of religion in ancient Egyptian culture. The pyramids of Menkaure (*left*) and Khafre (*center*) are also shown below.

HOW WERE THE ANCIENT EGYPTIANS RULED?

For thousands of years, Egypt was one of the most efficiently ruled states in the world. At the heart of its government was the king or, occasionally, the queen. Known in later times by the even grander title of "pharaoh" (*see page 11*), ancient Egyptian monarchs were considered more than just rulers. They were seen as living, godlike symbols of Egypt itself.

TWO BECOMES ONE

Egypt's civilization first flourished along the banks of the Nile River in southern (Upper) and northern (Lower) Egypt. These areas were occupied by various tribes, each with its own chief. Gradually, the many tribes came under a single leader for the north and another for the south. These leaders were perhaps the world's first kings.

Around 3100 B.C., the king of Upper Egypt conquered the north, or Lower Egypt, and became ruler of the whole country. Tradition says his name was Menes. Scholars believe this is myth and that the true first king of all Egypt was most likely King Narmer or King Aha.

THE DYNASTIES

King Aha was the first king of the first dynasty, or ruling family. This dynasty provided eight kings. It was followed by the second dynasty, with seven kings, and so on to the thirtieth dynasty almost three millennia later.

Dynasties did not always follow smoothly from each other. Occasionally there were rebellions and civil wars. These years are called "Intermediate Periods." Ancient Egypt suffered three of them: the First Intermediate Period (2181–2055 B.C.), the Second Intermediate Period (1650–1550 B.C.), and the Third Intermediate Period (1069–747 B.C.).

Between the Intermediate Periods were three periods known as "Kingdoms:" the Old Kingdom (2686–2181 B.C.), the Middle Kingdom (2055–1650 B.C.), and the New Kingdom (1550–1069 B.C.). Each had its dynasties and distinct cultural style. The country's most famous monuments, the Great Pyramid and the Sphinx, date from the Old Kingdom. We are best informed about the New Kingdom because it was the most recent and there is more evidence in existence from this period. It also provided some of Egypt's most famous monarchs, such as Ramses II (r. 1279–1213 B.C.).

▲ A detail from the painted casket of King Tutankhamen (c. 1370–1352 B.C.) shows the young king scattering his enemies while being cooled by the fans of his courtiers.

KING-GODS

Religion and ruling could not be separated in ancient Egypt. The king's job was to preserve harmony (*Maat*) on Earth, and because this harmony was thought to be god-given, the king therefore needed godlike powers. Thus, from the earliest times, the king was regarded as part-god.

Some early kings were thought of as actual gods, masters of the universe. After about 2180 B.C., the king's divine status on Earth became less certain. Nevertheless, after death, kings were believed to become actual gods. Their earthly title of pharaoh, in use by the New Kingdom, originally meant simply "great house," or royal palace. Over time, it came to mean the most important person from that palace— the king or ruling queen.

From an Egyptian account of the Battle of Qadesh:

"His majesty . . . arrayed himself in [put on] his coat of mail. He . . . charged into the foes of the vanquished chief . . . and the numerous countries which were with him. His majesty was . . . great in strength, smiting and slaying among them; his majesty hurled them headlong, one upon another."

What does it tell us?

At first glance, this quotation suggests that the king, Ramses II (the Great), was a brave warrior. Other evidence, however, indicates that the writer may have exaggerated Ramses' valor. The piece may be more valuable for showing how kings could have been flattered by members of their court—and promoted to their subjects—rather than for giving factual information.

Each king had five names. A king's name reinforced his status. His second name was always Horus, linking him to the falcon-god Horus, the protector of kingship. As the falcon flew high above the land, so the king was thought to soar over Egypt. Another mark of a king's importance is found in the Egyptian system of dates. Dates did not link one reign to another; instead, dates started with the first year of each new king, as if time itself began with each new ruler.

ALL-POWERFUL

The king was principal administrator, chief priest, and army commander, although in practice he usually handed down these functions to ministers, priests, and generals. Marriage customs were another sign of the king's remarkable status. Because of his god-like position, the king was not bound by normal social rules. His many wives, for example, could include his own sisters and daughters. In fact, the powerful Queen Hatshepsut was one of the wives of her brother, King Thutmose III.

In theory, the Double Crown of Upper and Lower Egypt, worn by kings after the unification of the country, passed down from father to son. In practice, things were not so simple. Some kings (such as Apepi II) were unimpressive; others probably devoted themselves more to personal pleasure than to the tasks of government. As a result of the activities

Appearing in royal glory

What does it tell us?

Ramses III emerged before his people in this high "window of appearances" in the temple-palace at Medinet Habu (*below*). The height shows how he wished to be seen: literally, above his subjects. This physical supremacy represented his semi-divine status. Also, the window faces east, toward the rising Sun, so the king would appear with the Sun shining upon him.

of incompetent rulers, Egyptian history is littered with stories of plot and rebellion. This allowed men like the talented Horemeb to climb from nothing to the highest position in the land. He joined the army, rose to become its

▲ The remains of the Mortuary Temple of Queen Hatshepsut found at Luxor, Egypt.

commander during the reign of Tutankhamen, and was eventually declared king in 1323 B.C.

Royal women always had power either as the king's mother, his chief wife, or one of his other wives. Some, such as Queen Nefertiti (died 1340 B.C.), became as powerful as the king himself. The most remarkable was powerful Hatshepsut (r. 1473–1458 B.C.), who ruled as queen and king (and was called pharaoh) while Thutmose III (c. 1479–1425 B.C.) was still a child. She is shown wearing the royal false beard, and inscriptions refer to her, remarkably, as "he."

Two crowns, one king

What does it tell us?

This sculpture shows the Double Crown of Upper and Lower Egypt. It reminds us that the king was known as "Lord of the Two Lands" and that Egypt had once been two kingdoms. The first kings are shown wearing just the white crown of Upper Egypt. When combined with the red crown of Lower Egypt, it produced the "Two Mighty Ones." The Double Crown shows that kings were eager to emphasize Egypt's unity.

Vizier Sinuhe meets the king:

"I found his majesty on the great throne in a kiosk of gold. Stretched out on my belly, I did not know myself before him . . . I was like a man seized by darkness . . . my heart was not in my body, I did not know life from death."

What does it tell us?

This extract suggests the fear with which a king was received, even by someone as important as a vizier. It also tells of the majesty of the king's surroundings. There is a possibility, however, that the vizier exaggerates his fear and the king's majesty in order to flatter his lord and master.

The mighty priest-king

What does it tell us?

This sculpture of the bust of King Amenemhet (1843–1798 B.C.) of the twelfth dynasty, in the robes of a high priest, indicates the many functions of a king. His religious role was rather complicated because he was more than just a priest—he was a semi-god himself. The Egyptians believed this gave him special powers to influence other gods on his subjects' behalf.

ADMINISTRATION

The leading officials beneath a king were his vizier (a sort of prime minister), his chief priests, and his buildings' managers. At the time of a king like Ramses II (the Great), who built an enormous number of monuments, the buildings' managers were second only to the king in importance. Also powerful were the military commanders. Thutmose III (died 1425 B.C.), a formidable soldier, took personal command of his armies, while Seti I (1294–1279 B.C.) relied on his vizier Amenemope to lead a successful campaign against the Nubians to the south.

At court, the vizier (of whom there were sometimes more than one) was assisted by a treasurer, chief steward, and other household officials. Royal power extended over the rest of the country through both a system of religious organization, run through the temples,

▲ A wall painting (c. 1400–1390 B.C.) shows two rope-stretchers marking out the boundaries of a field.

and another system for keeping law and order and seeing that taxes were paid. Under the second system, the kingdom was divided between Upper and Lower Egypt, then each part was further split up into districts called *nomes*.

A nome was looked after by an official called a *nomarch*. A nomarch was served by scribes who checked accounts, collected taxes (usually in the form of wheat), oversaw the law, and made sure fields were the correct size. Scribes called "rope-stretchers" marked out boundaries. Because the inundation washed away boundaries each year, fields had to be re-marked every autumn by using ropes as tape measures.

HOW DID EGYPT GET ALONG WITH ITS NEIGHBORS?

The Egyptians believed they were superior to all other people on Earth. It is not difficult to see why: They knew nothing of great civilizations elsewhere in the world, such as China, and their wealth, organization, and skills certainly made them appear more able than their neighbors. This feeling of superiority did not stop the Egyptians from having contact with those living beyond their borders, but not all of it was pleasant.

TRADE AND TRIBUTE

Two aspects of the Egyptians' way of life made trade difficult: They did not use money until late in the first millennium B.C., and, in theory, the state (the king) owned everything. Consequently, it is rare to hear of Egyptian traders or merchants operating on their own.

One of the country's best-known trading missions was that which Queen Hatshepsut (*see page 13*) sent down the Red Sea to the land of "Punt," which was

Egypt meets the wider world

What does it tell us?

This scene is carved on the walls of Pharaoh Hatshepsut's temple at Deir el-Bahri. It shows Egyptian traders in the land of Punt. They are laying out their goods while the people of Punt lay out theirs. The carving is excellent evidence for the type of goods traded, the fact that trade was important enough to be shown on a temple wall, and shows that trade was done by barter rather than with money.

somewhere on the coast of East Africa. The Egyptian ships took cloth, grain, papyrus, copper, and gems. They traded these for exotic products like myrrh (including whole myrrh trees), gold, ebony, ivory, wild animals (including baboons, which were sacred to the Egyptians), and slaves.

To the north, the Egyptians exchanged goods with the lands of the Eastern Mediterranean, while caravans of mules and donkeys carried merchandise back and forth across the desert to the west. As with their East African trade, Egypt's main products of exchange were grain and cloth. Egyptians imported timber,

spices, and some metals. Most goods were carried in foreign boats from ports such as Byblos in Lebanon, although, by the time of the New Kingdom, some Egyptian temples had fleets of their own to trade with.

Goods were traded in the monarch's name. Materials entering Egypt were labeled as "tribute" (offerings) from lesser peoples to the Great King. Goods going the other way were described as gifts to people "beyond respect." No foreign nation was admitted to have a king—he was called simply "chief" or "big man." The Egyptians claimed that only they had a true king.

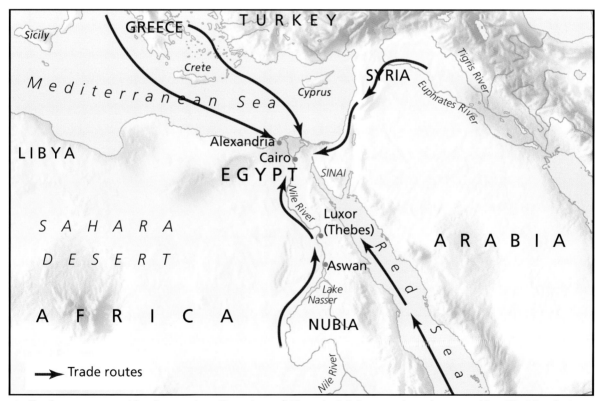

▲ Trade routes used by the ancient Egyptians. (When helpful, some locations are identified by their present names.)

WAR AND NUBIA

Wealthy Egypt was a tempting target for attackers. Its survival for 3,000 years shows its military as well as economic strength. By the time of the New Kingdom, it had a well-organized, permanent army of chariots and foot soldiers to defend and expand the frontiers. Favored weapons appear to have been spears. The infantry also carried leather shields, and the higher-ranking soldiers had body armor.

The most troublesome frontier was with Nubia (in present-day Sudan), the land to the south where the Nile makes a huge "S" bend. For many hundreds of years, the Nubians raided Egypt in search of precious loot. The Egyptians tried to conquer Nubia for its valuable gold, slaves, exotic African products, and the trade route to sub-Saharan Africa. At one point, Nubia (as the kingdom of Kush) conquered Egypt. Eventually, during the New Kingdom, the Egyptians overcame Nubia and built stout fortresses there to maintain control.

EMPIRE

Until around 1800 B.C., attacks on Egypt from the Mediterranean and across the Sinai Peninsula had been largely in the form of raids. During the Second Intermediate Period (*see page 10*), however, the Hyksos people from Syria-Palestine came to rule large parts of Egypt. The Egyptians regained this land

▼ A model of a Nile boat from the Middle Kingdom.

Ramses II – the mightiest of the mighty

What does it tell us?

This copy of an ancient Egyptian painting shows Ramses II galloping toward his enemies in a chariot. It gives the impression that he is triumphing over them without difficulty. Most kings, whether successful warriors or not, were shown in this way. The picture is designed to build up a powerful image of Ramses rather than record a historical event.

during the New Kingdom when they went on the attack and carved out an empire along the eastern seaboard of the Mediterranean. At its largest, under Thutmose I (1493–1482 B.C.), the empire reached from the Euphrates River in the north to Kurgus (in Sudan), in the south, and expanded west into Libya. The benefits of empire were enormous. Vast quantities of tribute poured into Egypt in the form of gold, silver, timber, spices, scents, and other commodities. The Egyptians had never known such wealth.

By the time of Ramses III (1184–1153 B.C.), the Egyptian Empire was in decline, and "Sea People" from the Aegean area threatened. Egyptian power collapsed further under Ramses' successors, until the country divided and fell to successive invaders and was finally absorbed into the Roman Empire in 30 B.C.

From a temple inscription at Medinet Habu: Ramses III records how he prepares for an attack of the "Sea People."

"I … prepared the river mouth like a strong wall with warships, galleys, and skiffs. They were completely equipped both fore and aft with brave fighters carrying their weapons and infantry of all the pick of Egypt, being like roaring lions upon the mountain."

What does it tell us?

This extract suggests many things. First, Ramses III clearly knew that the "Sea People" were coming and was therefore able to get his defenses ready. Second, at that time, Egypt had a navy, or at least seagoing ships that the king could use in time of war. Third, naval warfare seems to have been fought by ships carrying soldiers, like a land battle at sea.

WHAT WAS LIFE LIKE IN ANCIENT EGYPT?

It is not easy to imagine what everyday life was like in ancient Egypt. The Egyptians did not know about many things—electricity, for example—that we take for granted. Egyptians had no say in their government, and they did not have much idea of civilizations elsewhere. By our standards, most Egyptians lived short, tough, and poorly informed lives.

That said, certain pieces of evidence, such as a statue of a loving couple, remind us that we are basically the same as our distant Egyptian ancestors. Archaeologists have discovered many artifacts, from cooking vessels and toys to written tablets, paintings, and sculptures, that show us in great detail how Egyptians lived, worked, played, hunted, governed, studied, and made war.

Evidence under the desert

What does it tell us?

These are the remains of a village for workers digging royal graves in the Valley of the Kings. The site offers valuable information about the size, shape, and construction of houses. The density of the housing and the narrowness of the streets suggests that the community probably was well organized to manage matters like water and sewage. Unfortunately, we cannot tell how typical this village may have been.

What does it tell us?

This limestone carving of a house, dating from the Third Intermediate Period (1069–747 B.C.), is a valuable source of information on Egyptian domestic life. The small door and tiny, barred windows were probably like that for security reasons, which suggests burglary was common. Notice the flat roof above the ground floor, edged with a parapet. As there seems to be no door in the floor below, there probably was an outside stairway leading from ground level.

AT HOME

The royal families lived in grand palaces. Archaeological evidence suggests that these were huge buildings with many rooms to accommodate the king's family, courtiers, servants, and slaves. Public rooms were decorated with tiles and paintings. At the heart of the palace, in a hall of many pillars, the king's throne stood on a raised platform. Wealthy families lived in spacious villas with enclosed gardens and pools of cooling water. Like the palaces, the interior walls were brightly painted and the floors laid with colored tiles.

Little is known about the homes of ordinary people. The Egyptians thought they were not worth describing in words or pictures, and over the millennia they have either been pulled down or have largely crumbled away. From models, remaining foundations, and lower parts of walls, it seems that ordinary houses were made of mud brick. The windows were tiny and there usually were no more than four rooms at ground level. Experts believe that they used the roof for storage and sleeping in hot weather. The houses of ordinary people probably were dark and bleak inside, with little decoration or furniture. Excavated ruins show that there often were brick benches around the walls, some wooden three-legged stools with rush or leather seats, and a low table. Pegs on the walls and baskets woven from reeds, as well as wheel-made pottery, provided storage. Egyptians cooked in cylindrical clay stoves or outside over open fires.

Nebamun hunting

What does it tell us?

This picture, painted on the tomb of the scribe Nebamun (died 1352 B.C.), shows him hunting with a throwing stick. His wife, at the rear of the boat, and his daughter, holding her father's leg, look on. The family cat goes into the reeds after the birds Nebamun has hit. The painting is excellent evidence on hunting practices; the types of birds caught, such as ducks; and even dress and jewelry (although Nebamun's wife seems a bit over-dressed for a hunting trip).

MEALTIME

The basic diet of most Egyptians was bread, vegetables, and fruit. They made their bread from barley or a grain known as emmer wheat. They also made cakes and pastries from these grains, and used barley for brewing beer. They baked bread on the outside surface of tall pottery ovens in which fires burned. The loaves were flat, round, and rather tough.

▶ A relief carving of a man fishing in the marshes of the Nile River with a net.

Common vegetables were lentils and other beans, leeks, onions, and lettuce. Melons, figs, and dates grew on the riverbank and in orchards irrigated by its waters. Pomegranates were a special luxury reserved for the wealthy or for feast days. Herbs and spices livened up dull meals, while cooking oil was crushed from plants such as flax. Milk and cheese were not plentiful.

The Nile provided fresh fish, especially perch, and people living on the coast had an even wider variety of catch. Poorer families did not eat meat regularly. Many kept goats for milk, cheese, and wool, and geese (for eggs). Some temples owned a herd of cattle, which were valuable animals; sheep and pigs also were rare. This meant beef, lamb, and pork were luxuries. More common was meat the Egyptians got by hunting the ducks and geese that lived in the Nile marshes.

Bread, fish, vegetables, fruit: The diet of the average Egyptian was certainly very healthy. None of their food was processed, and the fat content was very low. Most of it was fresh because the Egyptians could preserve it only by drying it in the sun, pickling it, smoking, or salting it. The dry climate meant that grain could be stored without going rotten, although rodents and insects were a constant problem.

Edible evidence

What does it tell us?

This Egyptian wall painting of servants bringing food for a feast gives a fair idea of the range of food eaten at the time. As well as fruits (including grapes and pomegranates), there are summer squash, huge fish, ducks, and geese. The man at the top has a string of small fish that, because they are to be served at a feast, may have been a delicacy. Note how all the food is fresh and makes up a well-balanced diet.

PARTY TIME

The Egyptians liked a good party. Feasts usually were religious, either to thank a deity for a personal benefit, such as the birth of a healthy child, or as part of a public festival. For a feast, the guests dressed in their best clothes and jewels, and applied their makeup with care. Entertainment was provided by speakers and singers, musicians, dancers, jugglers, and jesters.

Beer was the favorite alcoholic beverage. Egyptians made beer by fermenting barley and barley loaves. They also were wine experts. They made their wine from several grape varieties and stored it in labeled jars like modern-day wine bottles. As well as homemade wine, the

Party time!

What does it tell us?

This picture, painted on the wall of a tomb at Thebes, gives us details of dancing girls, a pipe player, women's dress, braided hair, and jewelry. More mysterious are the strange objects on the ladies' heads. Some experts used to think that these were cones of scented wax that released perfume as they melted. Scholars now suggest they may just represent goodness or holiness, as do halos in Christian and other religious pictures.

▲ An ancient Egyptian wall painting of a grape-picking scene.

wealthier people drank rich wines imported from the lands of the eastern Mediterranean, such as the land of Lebanon.

Festivals took place around and on the Nile. In the Opet Festival, the statue of Amun was hauled upstream from Karnak to Luxor in a mysterious ritual that reconfirmed royal power. The Festival of the Beautiful Embrace celebrated the union of Horus and Hathor. This festival took the form of a marriage between the two deities. The statue of Hathor was taken to meet the statue of Horus, where an act called the "beautiful embrace" took place.

Extract from the Story of the Deities Isis and Osiris:

"In celebration, Seth . . . held a spectacular feast at his city of Tanis . . . Tales were told, boasts exchanged, dances performed, and much beer was consumed."

What does it tell us?

Because Egyptians believed their gods and goddesses had many human characteristics, the writer gives his story a human setting. The piece suggests many things about the customs at Egyptian feasts. It reveals, for example, that beer was drunk and that dancing was an entertainment. Furthermore, it seems evident that the guests enjoyed storytelling and boastful conversation.

▲ This wall painting, from 1400–1390 B.C., shows elegant ladies at a concert.

GETTING DRESSED

During the 3,000 years of Egyptian civilization, clothing styles remained surprisingly similar. Everyday wear for ordinary people hardly changed at all. Working men wore a loincloth made of linen or leather, and women wore a straight-sided sheath dress with straps across the shoulders. Nakedness was not frowned upon among the children and slaves, who often were shown in ancient Egyptian art wearing no clothes at all.

Formal menswear consisted of a kind of kilt, which by the New Kingdom was pleated. By the first millennium B.C., it had become baggier than before. Art also shows evidence of men wearing linen shirts. Women's dresses evolved from two shoulder straps to one. Later, Greek designs became fashionable with more richly colored materials and fuller dresses. Wealthier men and women wore sandals woven from papyrus.

Linen was the most usual material for clothes, although cotton cloth also was available. The time-consuming, skilled business of spinning threads and then weaving them into cloth was done mostly by women. All articles of clothing were handmade at home. Once a woman had spun enough thread, she would string it onto a loom, weave other threads back and forth across the loom's warp threads, and then sew the garment together.

LOOKING GOOD

If their illustrations are realistic, the guests at an Egyptian party must have looked stunning. Wealthy men and women wore thick, black wigs over their shaved heads and adorned themselves with rings, earrings, and bands on arms, ankles, and wrists. They also wore huge collars of glittering gold and precious stones. Gold and silver were expensive, so ordinary people made do with copper and bronze. Onyx, garnet, and amethyst were popular gemstones found in Egypt.

One of the more exotic features of Egyptian pictures is the heavy eye makeup shown on men and women, indicating that Egyptians commonly used such makeup on themselves. They used kohl, a dark liner made from lead and oil, to make their eyes look bigger and to protect their eyes from the glare of the Sun. Nail paint and coloring for the cheeks and lips were also used.

A limestone bust ▶ displays the ancient beauty: Queen Nefertiti, wife of King Akhenaton, from c. 1340 B.C.

MOM, DAD, AND THE KIDS

Egyptian society was based on the family, and everyday work revolved around the home. The father was head of the family, but women definitely were not second-class citizens. They managed the household and were regarded as equal to men in the law courts. Parents left their possessions to both male and female children. Women rarely did the tough manual work that men did, although they might help their husbands with the farming. A few women had very influential positions: Before the New Kingdom, women priests served in temples, and exceptional queens, such as Hatshepsut, exercised their royal power.

As far as we know, Egyptians did not have formal marriage ceremonies. A couple simply set up house together and shared responsibilities. The common age for doing this was about thirteen for girls and fifteen for boys. Only male members of the royal family (who were allowed to break all the rules!) had more than one wife. Couples might split up if they failed to have children. When this happened, relatives and friends made sure that each was treated fairly.

Children were highly prized. Many spells, potions, and medicines were available to help a couple conceive. Although children seem to have been well cared for, childhood was short. Young people

from ordinary backgrounds would be expected to help around the house or farm as soon as they were able, and by the age of ten they would be thinking of an independent future.

Grave evidence

What does it tell us?

This painted wooden chest used for storing makeup products belonged to Kha, the Director of Works at Deir-el-Medina, and his wife. Found in their tomb, the artifacts remind us that Egyptians were buried with everyday goods they believed would be needed in the Afterlife. The find also reveals the skills of a range of Egyptian craft workers, including carpenters, painters, potters, and cosmetics manufacturers. Wood was scarce and expensive in Egypt, so the box also tells us that Kha must have been fairly wealthy.

Happy family

The parents on the left of this wall painting (c. 1198–1166 B.C.) are surrounded by their children while servants bring food and drink. The picture clearly illustrates the long wigs worn by both men and women, and the hairstyles of children. Most prominent is the "side-lock of youth," a piece of hair left growing from an otherwise shaven head. Notice that it was considered normal, in this hot climate, for children to go about naked. Egyptian artists typically exaggerated the smaller size of children and also of servants and less important people and usually showed faces in profile.

UPHOLDING MAAT

Ancient Egyptian law is a bit mysterious to us because right and wrong were based on *Maat*—the religious idea of balance and harmony. Only in the first millennium B.C. was the law formally written down. Before then, it seems that any official—the vizier, for example— could act as judge over someone accused of disrupting Maat. The king was the highest judge. Many local cases were heard by councils of more important citizens. Occasionally, a god was asked to give a judgement, although it is not known how a god made his or her decision known.

One of the harshest punishments for upper-class Egyptians was exile— being sent out of the country. Fines, prison, and beatings were used for lesser crimes. More serious breaches of Maat were punished harshly with mutilation of the criminal's body— cutting out the tongue or severing a hand or ear. The ultimate punishment was death. The luckier criminals were simply beheaded or drowned. The less fortunate had wooden stakes rammed through their bodies or were burned alive. Not only that: It was assumed that the gods would continue to punish the criminals in the next world for having disturbed the heavenly balance of Maat on Earth.

SLAVES

As in almost all ancient civilizations, the Egyptians had slaves. These usually were prisoners of war or foreigners obtained by trading. A slave was not seen as a person at all, but as a useful animal—like a mule or a cat. Slaves lacked rights, so owners could treat slaves as they wished.

This might give a rather gloomy picture of life as a slave. In fact, only the slaves who worked in mines were treated horribly. Others might be soldiers or, best of all, household servants. Much depended on their masters and mistresses, but in a kind family it was sometimes possible for a slave to live a fairly comfortable life.

◀ This bronze figurine from 1450–1340 B.C. shows a slave bound hand and foot.

Backbreaking work

What does it tell us?

In this wall painting of workers in the fields, men sow seeds from a basket and hoe with short-handled instruments. This picture tells us something about agriculture in ancient Egypt: The soil deposited by inundation was so light and rich that it did not need to be plowed before sowing. Instead, it usually was plowed or hoed after sowing in order to cover the seeds lying on the surface.

Magistrates report the work of tomb robbers during the reign of Ramses IX:

"The sepulcher of the king, golden Sun of the creation, son of the Sun, Imhotep . . . was found to have been broken into. (The thieves) had advanced two and a half cubits (a cubit is the distance from the elbow to the tip of one's fingers) . . . This is the only damage."

What does it tell us?

A thief who tackled a royal shrine risked curses, a terrible death if caught, and certain damnation after death—yet the thieves still went ahead. This would suggest that perhaps not all ancient Egyptians believed in their country's religious system, with the monarch at its head—or perhaps, in some cases, poverty posed a greater threat than punishment.

HOW DID THE EGYPTIANS COMMUNICATE?

There were two types of education in ancient Egypt: practical and academic. Very few children—less than 1 in 200—received an academic education. For most Egyptians, "education" meant learning to do what their parents did.

This elegantly illustrated *Book of the Dead*, ▼ with its hieroglyphs, shows a funeral.

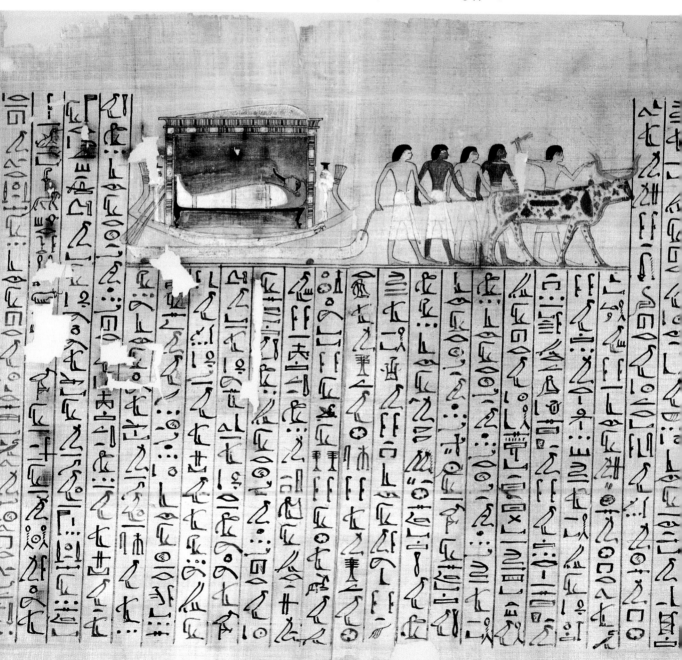

The key that unlocked the past

What does it tell us?

The famous Rosetta Stone is the archaeological discovery that helped crack the code of Egyptian writing. It was found in Rosetta, Egypt, in 1799. The key to the code was that the carved text presents the same subject matter in three writing systems: ancient Greek, demotic, and hieroglyphic (the latter two forms were used by the ancient Egyptians). In 1822, the brilliant French scholar, Jean-Francois Champollion, used his knowledge of ancient Greek to become the first person to decode ancient Egyptian writing.

APPRENTICESHIP

Almost all boys learned their fathers' occupations and skills and continued this work when their fathers died. They became apprenticed to their fathers (or to some other close male relative) at about the age of ten and began to learn on the job. Education usually involved picking up agricultural skills, such as sowing, harvesting, and threshing.

During the inundation season (*see page 6*), farmers went to work on government projects, such as building temples. Their sons went with them and learned other skills—perhaps brick-making or even carving. Highly skilled craftsmen, such as painters, generally worked at their trade all year round and did not farm, and neither did their sons.

Girls followed much the same pattern as boys, except that they shadowed their mothers in order to learn about work set aside for women. They began their apprenticeship earlier than boys, perhaps starting at the age of eight. The sort of skills they acquired were baby care, cooking, spinning, weaving, and growing fruits and vegetables.

SCHOOLING

Schools, which were only for the upper classes, were attached to important buildings, such as temples or palaces. As far as we know, only boys had formal schooling, although some scholars believe a few aristocratic women also learned to write. We cannot be sure because the examples of women's writing we have may have been dictated by women but written down by men. Many people relied on scribes to write important documents and letters for them.

Lessons were strict, with plenty of corporal punishment, and were often boring. The main way of learning was copying something many times and memorizing it. Boys were taught reading, writing, and mathematics. The latter was extremely practical, with no abstract theories. The system was decimal, with signs for one, ten, one hundred, and so on up to one million. (The numeral for one million meant "I can't count this far!") They had no numeral for zero. Literacy was taught by scribes, who were among the most important people in Egyptian society. Scribes were not just people who knew how to read and write. Because they possessed those rare skills, they were managers, accountants, officials, and organizers. All government business depended on the work of scribes.

Driving a royal scribe

What does it tell us?

This is a carving of the Royal Scribe Ani being driven in his chariot by a slave. One of his titles was Accounting Scribe for the Divine Offerings of All the Gods. His clothing, the personal chariot, and the very fact that this image of him was made at all indicate his wealth and importance. Scribes like Ani were usually more like modern government officials than just writers.

WRITING

The first Egyptian writing system developed from pictures. These pictures were simplified into standard shapes, or hieroglyphs. By the time of the New Kingdom, about 1,000 of these symbols existed. Signs also represented ideas and

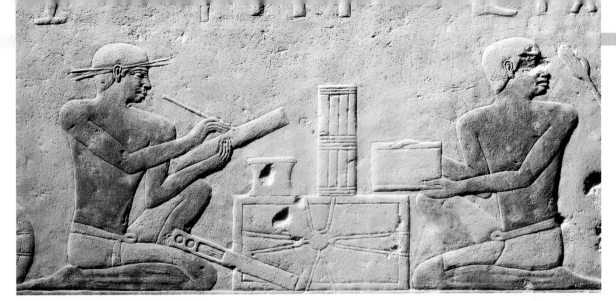

▲ This bas-relief sculpture shows two scribes at work, from c. 2494–2345 B.C.

sounds. Some key elements of Egyptian writing were not standardized. For example, the writing could go from left to right, or right to left, top to bottom, or bottom to top, with no punctuation or gaps between words. Not surprisingly, scholars puzzled for centuries to figure out what it all meant.

Experts believe that hieroglyphic writing was deliberately kept difficult so that only those specially trained could read it. This kept power in the hands of the small minority of educated people. Egyptians also thought symbols could be dangerous: They believed a picture of something had the power of the thing itself.

Because use of hieroglyphs was slow and complex, it usually was reserved for formal documents and inscriptions. For everyday writing, an easier system was developed—hieratic script. This system had a business form and a literary form.

From the business form emerged an even simpler style known as demotic script. Even this was complicated, however, and during Roman times all forms of hieroglyph became obsolete.

King Amenmessu writes advice to his son

"Here begins the teaching which the late King of Upper and Lower Egypt . . . made when he spoke in imparting [giving] truth to his son . . ."

What does it tell us?

This is the introduction to a document in which King Amenmessu gives advice to his son. Because there are many documents like this, such written teachings may have been designed to be part of an heir's education. Boys had to copy these teachings, which helped their writing skills. The content of the document also was important, since it passed on the father's wisdom to his son.

WHO DID THE ANCIENT EGYPTIANS WORSHIP?

A ncient Egyptian religion was tremendously important and extremely complicated. It was important because the king and his subjects believed it was a matter of life or death—not just for individual people but for the whole Earth. It was complicated because, unlike Judaism, Christianity, or Islam, it had not been established with a basic set of teachings. Egyptian religion developed over thousands of years and in different parts of the country.

PRESERVING HARMONY

The Egyptians believed everything existed in opposites, such as good/bad, order/chaos, life/death, and Egyptians/barbarians. Religion's purpose was to make sure that the good outweighed the bad; in other words, religion had to ward off chaos (*Isfet*) and maintain peace, justice, truth, and harmony (Maat). Doing this required pleasing the gods and goddesses that controlled the world.

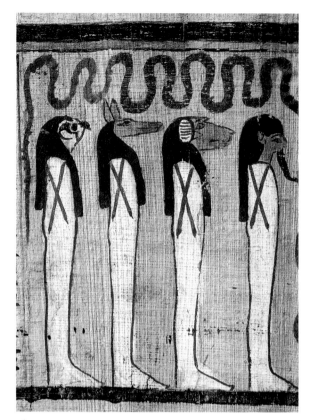

▲ Experts believe these images from the *Book of the Dead* of Heruben show the gods (*left to right*) Horus, Anubis, Khnum, and Ptah.

Because the Egyptians thought their deities had human and/or animal characteristics, the faithful believed they needed looking after physically rather than just through good words and thoughts or prayer. Tending the gods and goddesses was the purpose of the temples, in which Egyptians believed their gods lived. Failure to please a deity, the Egyptians feared, led to punishment. Punishment might be minor, like breaking an arm; but it also could be nationwide, such as a plague or drought. Egyptians felt that this system of beliefs explained all that went on in the world.

If foreigners invaded, for example, the Egyptians believed they were being punished for annoying a powerful deity, such as the falcon-god Horus. Because they believed that their religion explained and affected everything, the Egyptians believed there was no difference between religion, magic, and science.

CREATION

A good example of the complexity of Egyptian religion is how it explained creation. The beginning of the world has always bewildered humankind. The Jewish, Christian, and Muslim traditions talk of a Creator, the Garden of Eden, and so on. The Egyptians had three main creation stories, each originating in different parts of the country and at different times.

The creation story from Hermopolis Magna said the first thing to appear was the Sun-disk god (Aten), mysteriously created by eight deities of chaos. The Heliopolis story said the Sun-god created himself with the aid of magic, then used his bodily fluids to make further new life. A third story was popular at Memphis. It said that the creator-god Ptah made all things by speaking their names. Even more confusing, the Egyptians believed creation did not happen just once but went on all the time—for example, the Sun "died" every evening and was "reborn" each morning.

Glorious even in death

What does it tell us?

This small gold coffin was created c. 1347–1337 B.C. It held the preserved internal organs of King Tutankhamen and was discovered in 1922 at Tutankhamen's largely unspoiled tomb in the Valley of the Kings. The fact that such a beautiful and precious object was made to contain the internal organs of the young king's body shows how important preserving a body was to the ancient Egyptians, and, perhaps, how much the boy was loved. This coffin also reflects Tutankhamen's wealth and shows the amazing skills of Egyptian craft workers. Although the king's face may not be realistic, the carving provides information about the royal headdress and false beard, which typically was tied on with string in real life.

▲ This broken sculpture still reveals a strong portrait of the head of King Akhenaton.

GODS AND GODDESSES

Two important Egyptian deities were Amun, "the hidden one," and the Sun-god Ra. During the New Kingdom, they often were joined together as the super-deity Amun-Ra. King Akhenaton (1352–1336 B.C.) proclaimed the Sun-disk god Aten as the supreme and only god, but the idea of a single deity did not catch on, and the Egyptians soon went back to their old multi-deity system.

Three other popular deities were Osiris, Isis, and Horus. Osiris was the mummy god of death, birth, and rebirth. He and his sister-partner Isis had a son Horus, the falcon-god associated with the kings. A god originally associated with specific places was the crocodile-god Sobek. In time, he became so popular that some kings, including Sobekneferu (1799–1795 B.C.) added his name to theirs.

One of the leading household gods was Taweret, shown as a female hippopotamus. She had large breasts and, sometimes, the limbs of a lion and the tail of a crocodile. A kindly deity, Taweret

From a Book of the Dead on the Papyrus of Ani (1240 B.C.):

"I have not done falsehood [lied] against men, I have not impoverished my associates . . . I have not deprived the orphan of his property."

What does it tell us?

A copy of the *Book of the Dead* was buried with a body to help it pass through the Underworld. They consisted of spells and chants to please Osiris, the judge of the dead. The chants quoted above show that, like modern religions, the beliefs of the ancient Egyptians encouraged them to lead good lives on Earth so they might be rewarded in the Afterlife.

Part of a hymn to Aten:

"Thou appearest beautifully on the horizon of heaven, Thou living Aten, the beginning of life! When thou art risen on the eastern horizon, Thou hast filled every land with thy beauty."

What does it tell us?

Aten was the Sun-disk god. Some believe he was the Sun itself. The song suggests the importance of the Sun in Egyptian society—it brought light and warmth and enabled crops to grow. Because of this, many people believed it was obviously a god. The daily rising of the Sun also was believed to be like the rebirth of a person after his or her earthly life.

looked after women in childbirth. She did not have her own temples but was thought to live in carvings on amulets and in her statues in many homes.

TEMPLES AND RITUALS

The Egyptians believed that a temple was often a deity's home. According to their religion, the spirit of a deity lived in a statue in the sanctuary at the heart of the temple. Three times a day, priests cleaned the statue, dressed it in new clothes and jewelry, and left it fresh food. By doing this, the priests hoped the deity would remain contentedly within their temple. Priests could be full-time or part-time. They had to keep scrupulously clean and shave off all bodily hair—even their eyebrows and eyelashes. Originally, some temples were served by priestesses as well as priests, but, by the New Kingdom, priests had taken over completely. Nevertheless, women still participated in worship by singing in temple choirs.

▲ This relief sculpture of Sobek, the Egyptian crocodile-god, was taken from Kom Ombo Temple, built during the Ptolemaic period.

THE AFTERLIFE

In the ancient Egyptian religion, the death of the earthly body was just a phase of a person's life. People believed they would be able to go on living in a different form after death, and if they did things right, their new life might be enjoyable. Bodies were mummified to preserve them for use in the Afterlife. People were buried with other things they might need, such as clothes and jewels.

The Egyptians believed that after earthly death, a person entered the long, dark, and scary corridors of the Underworld. If they found their way through (helped by a *Book of the Dead*), they were judged by Osiris. Those who passed the test became holy spirits and lived forever in happiness. The hearts of those who failed were thrown to the crocodile-lion-hippopotamus "Swallowing Monster." When a heart was swallowed, its owner ceased to exist.

Bes the friendly beast

What does it tell us?

This bronze sculpture is of the household god Bes. He is often shown standing on a lotus flower. He had an ugly face, but he was very popular. The Egyptians probably thought his ugliness was necessary because he scared snakes away from their houses. The lotus was the flower of Upper Egypt and a symbol of life and rebirth. Its association with Bes reminds us that Egyptians believed he would help with conception and all areas of human reproduction.

Protected by the jackal-god

What does it tell us?

This painting shows a priest wearing the mask of Anubis, the jackal-headed god of the dead and embalming. Anubis was seen as a guardian of places where the dead lay. Why did the Egyptians give the god a jackal head? Jackals were known to dig up and eat dead bodies; people hoped the jackal-god would stop this from happening. Another mystery about Anubis: Why is he black, when real jackals are brown? The answer may be that the god was given the color either of a mummified body or of night, when the Sun "died" and needed to be reborn. As a doglike god, Anubis also made an ideal guardian of places where the dead lay.

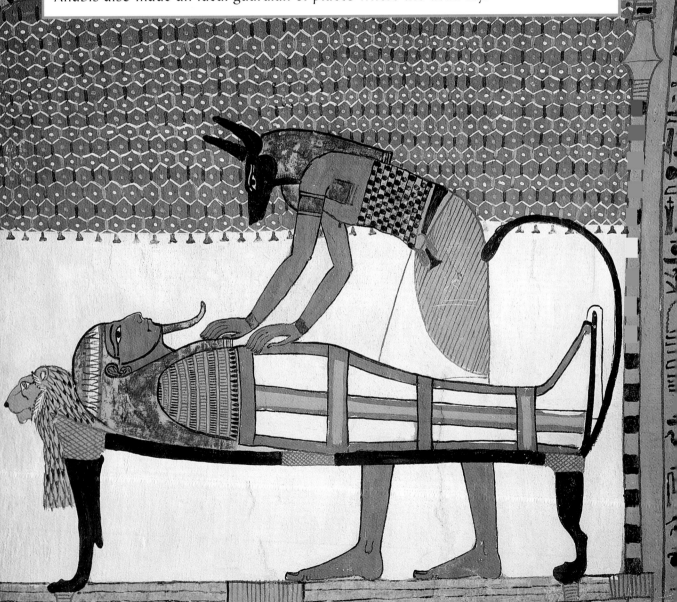

WHAT DID ANCIENT EGYPTIANS CONTRIBUTE TO THE WORLD?

The ancient Egyptians were a proud people. They believed themselves superior to other nations but had little wish to spread their way of life. Nevertheless, aspects of Egyptian culture were adopted by other civilizations, and some influence our world today.

The Egyptians gave us most of our basic measurements of time. The Egyptian calendar was based upon close observation of the Sun, moon, and stars. They were the first people to come up with a year of 365 days. Because an actual year is slightly longer (which is why we have leap years), working out ancient Egyptian dates is extremely difficult—especially as their year began in July, and dates started over again with the reign of each new king!

The twenty-four-hour day is another Egyptian invention. They also devised the water clock to measure daily time. Dealing with longer periods of time, Egyptian months were not quite like they are today. Although Egyptians had twelve months in a year, each one was thirty days long. This left five spare days, which they used for religious festivals.

The Abbott Papyrus—an investigation into tomb robberies

"Year 15, 19th Athor, was the day when Sha-em-djemi, governor of the town, and Nasiamen, official of the king, scribe of the court, proceeded to the examination of the main sites of the royal family . . . "

What does it tell us?

This extract shows an example of how the Egyptian calendar was used. Scholars have determined that "Year 15" is the fifteenth year of the reign of King Ramses IX. "19th Athor" is the nineteenth day of the month, named for the goddess Athor.

Stargazing also led the Egyptians to believe in the power and influence of "star signs," such as the ones we know as Aries, Taurus, and Pisces. These were introduced into Egypt from Babylon in the last millennium B.C. Today, as in ancient Egypt, millions of people still believe their lives are influenced by the heavenly bodies visible in the night sky.

ARCHITECTURE

Until modern times, the most famous design in Egyptian building, the pyramid, did not have much impact outside Egypt. The soaring stone columns found in temples and palaces, on the other hand, influenced the ancient Greeks in their Doric style of building. This, in turn, influenced Roman architecture, which featured columns supporting stone beams.

The Greco-Roman (classical) style of building then fell into disuse before being reintroduced at the time of the Renaissance. Since then, it has never really gone out of fashion. Many famous buildings of the modern world, such as the Capitol in Washington, D.C., show the influence of designs that began in ancient Egypt.

Evidence set in stone

What does it tell us?

The photograph below shows part of the temple of Amun that King Amenhotep III (c.1390-1352 B.C.) built at Luxor. The stone columns, with blocks at the top supporting heavy cross beams, are not so different from the columns found in ancient Greek buildings of the first millennium B.C. This sort of design is evident in some more "modern" buildings, such as the Parthenon in Athens. This shows the worldwide influence of ancient Egyptian architecture.

The last judgement

What does it tell us?

According to ancient Egyptian mythology, the soul of a person who has died is weighed against the feather of truth to see whether he or she has lived an honest life. If the two balance, the person goes to heaven; if the soul is heavier, the person is condemned to hell. This detail of the *Judgment of the Dead* painting on papyrus illustrates this myth. The idea of judgement preceding heaven or hell appears in later faiths, such as Christianity, and may be part of the complex religious legacy of ancient Egypt.

MEDICINE

In medicine, as in all other areas of life, the Egyptians did not distinguish between science and religion. Their medicine was what we would call a mixture of reason and magic. This mix did not stop it from being very advanced for its time. Egyptian doctors, especially in Alexandria, were respected by the Greeks, who were among the pioneers of modern scientific medicine.

Scholars believe that, by the first millennium B.C., some Egyptian doctors had areas of expertise, such as women's medicine. A remarkable document of about 1600 B.C. (found in 1862 by Egyptologist Edwin Smith) is a detailed

▲ Egyptian women made herbal medicines.

OTHER CONTRIBUTIONS

Because all of Egyptian civilization depended upon irrigation of dry land, ancient Egyptians pioneered many techniques of moving and preserving water for agriculture. One of their most enduring inventions was the *shaduf*. This hand-operated device raises water from a lower to a higher level. Shaped like a seesaw—with a skin or bucket at one end and a counterweight at the other end to raise the bucket—small shadufs are still used in modern Egypt.

account of ailments and how they should be treated. Some experts believe the author of the work, known—after its discoverer—as the Edwin Smith Medical Papyrus, even understood that blood circulated through the body, even though it would be some 3,000 years before this was scientifically proved.

Other ancient Egyptian medical documents deal with subjects such as pregnancy and contraception. One Egyptian pregnancy test, using wheat, has been shown to be remarkably accurate. Another medical text prescribes the best medicine for someone bitten by a hippopotamus! Few Egyptian remedies would make much sense to us today, but the attitude behind some of them—that disease, injury, and cure can be approached rationally—lies at the heart of modern medicine.

Egyptian art, especially its statues, influenced the work of Greek sculptors. Since the nineteenth century, Egyptian artistic styles have been copied in the West, too. Some scholars believe that the popular Egyptian image of Isis and her baby Horus (*see below*) was the inspiration for Christian pictures and statues of the Virgin Mary and the infant Jesus. The two images are often similar in style and design. With its rich legacy of artifacts, Egypt continues to give us glimpses into its glorious past.

◀ A bronze statue shows the goddess Isis and her baby Horus.

TIME LINE

All dates are B.C. and approximate.

7000–5500	Neolithic Age
5500–3150	Predynastic Period
	•Badarians settle in Upper Egypt
	•Hieroglyphic writing begins
3150–2690	Archaic Period (Dynasties 1–2)
2686–2181	Old Kingdom (Dynasties 3–6)
	•Sphinx and Great Pyramid at Giza built
	•Wars against Nubians, Libyans
2181–2055	First Intermediate Period (Dynasties 7–10)
2055–1650	Middle Kingdom (Dynasties 11–14)
	•King Mentuhotep reunites divided Egypt
1650–1550	Second Intermediate Period (Dynasties 15–17)
	•Horses introduced
	•Bronze used
1550–1069	New Kingdom (Dynasties 18–20)
	•Reigns of Hatshepsut, Thutmose III, and Tutankhamen
	•Tombs built in the Valley of the Kings
	•Temple of Amenhotep III built at Luxor
	•Reigns of Ramses II and III
1069–747	Third Intermediate Period (Dynasties 21–24)
	•Conquest by Nubians
747–332	Late Period (Dynasties 25–30)
	•Conquest by Assyrians and Persians
323–305	Conquest by Alexander the Great
	•Ptolemaic Dynasty
30	Egypt is absorbed into the Roman Empire

FIND OUT MORE

BOOKS

Biesty, Stephen. *Ancient Egypt.* OUP, 2005.

Deary, Terry. *The Awesome Egyptians.* Horrible Histories (series). Scholastic, Inc., 1997.

Ghali, Eda S. *Tales from Ancient Egypt.* Egypt and the Ancient World (series). Amidist, 1994.

Pipe, Jim. *Pharaoh's Tomb.* Copper Beech, 1997.

Hart, George. *Ancient Egypt.* Dorling Kindersley, 2004.

Allen, Anthony. *Pharaohs and Pyramids.* Usborne, 2004.

Wilkinson, Richard H. *The Complete Gods and Goddesses of Ancient Egypt.* Thames and Hudson, 2003.

WEB SITES

www.ancientegypt.co.uk/menu.html
Let the British Museum show you ancient Egypt.

www.bbc.co.uk/history/ancient/egyptians
Trace Egyptian history, listen to actors bring Egyptian letters to life, and more.

www.guardians.net/egypt
Enter the pyramids of Egypt and learn more about the pharaohs.

www.historyforkids.org/learn/egypt
Learn how to make Egyptian costumes and explore key components of Eygptian culture.

www.horus.ics.org.eg/en/default.aspx
Egyptians provide a guided tour of Egypt.

GLOSSARY

amulet—magic charm worn by the living or the dead to ward off evil

archaeology—studying the past by searching for and examining physical remains

barter—exchange goods rather than buy and sell them for money

bronze—metal made by mixing copper and tin

caravan—group of merchants traveling together on horses, camels, or mules

chant—type of religious singing

civilizations—settled communities of people who share a common, usually highly developed and literate, culture

courtier—person attending the royal court

deity—god or goddess

delta—mouth of a river that spreads into several channels where it enters the sea

divine—relating to a god or goddess

drought—time of no rainfall and severe water shortage when crops usually fail

dynasty—ruling family, or time when a single family rules

ebony—a hard, dark, highly valued wood

empire—several lands under the rule of an emperor or empress

export—to sell and send goods from one country to another

ferment—an aging process that produces alcohol in some liquids

hieroglyph—ancient Egyptian symbol used as a form of writing

inscription—short piece of writing, often carved in stone

Intermediate Period—time when Egypt's government was weak, marked by disorder and sometimes by invasion

inundation—flood, which was annual in Egypt

irrigation—large-scale watering of fields

kohl—dark eyeliner

Lower Egypt—northern Egypt

Maat—balance and harmony of all creation

millennium—one thousand years

mummy—corpse preserved by drying and treating with chemicals

nomarch—provincial governor in charge of a nome

nome—district

Nubia—region of present-day northern Sudan

papyrus—tough river reed from which the Egyptians made a type of paper— also called papyrus—from which they also made shoes

pharaoh—originally the king's "great house;" later used to mean the person from the great house—the king himself

Renaissance—movement in arts, science, and culture that occurred in Western Europe from the late fourteenth century into the seventeenth century; associated with new interest in ancient Greece and Rome, it marked a transition from medieval to modern times

ritual—significant religious action or rite repeated over and over again

sanctuary—inner chamber in a church or temple

scribe—someone able to read and write who usually performs this as a service for others

shrine—place where a god or goddess is worshipped

sphinx—mythical creature with a human head on the body of a lion

Stone Age—period of human development before the discovery of metals

tribute—payment of money or goods made to please a superior power, such as a king or an emperor

Upper Egypt—southern Egypt

vizier important minister or adviser

INDEX